FOR YOU, LOVE ALWAYS

COLLECTED POEMS

BRAEDEN MICHAELS

STORM & INK

2022

This book is an original work of poetry.

Copyright 2022 by Braeden Michaels

First paperback edition October 2022

Front cover design by bookcoverzone.com

ISBN 978-1-7347499-8-4 (paperback)

Published by Storm of Ink
PO Box 152
Gainesville, GA USA 30503
www.braedenmichaels.com

DEDICATION

The older I become, the more I realize I have more in my life that I could ever imagine. Often when we are young it's difficult to visualize what your life will be like in twenty years. It's hard to imagine who you will marry, how many kids you will have, or where you live.

After my first marriage I had to do some soul searching. My soul searching wasn't about my occupation, social status, or the possessions I owned. I thought about my dreams as a child. When I found my current wife, all the other things fell into place. I found a beautiful loving wife that believed in me. Without that, I would not be where I am today. I have a wife and son that are the center pieces of my life in Georgia. She took a chance on me in more ways than one. When I found her, I discovered myself.

As the years go on, often I wake up and really look at my surroundings. I embrace every second I have with my family. I am not a perfect husband or a perfect man, but I strive to be better. I have learned so much from my wife and son.

Thank you for your love and affection. Thank you for your patience, warmth, and the glowing heart you possess. Thank you for being you. Thank you for the woman you were when we met and the woman you are today. Thank you for being the light in my life.

TABLE OF CONTENTS

THE SUNFLOWER'S BREEZE

I fell between the pages of an old love story,
where the fears drip from a morning hymn
clouds are reckless and cliches are terrified
I found myself captivated by the nuances,
echoes of solace bellow and the dreams
in her hand disperse out into the nightfall

You are the comfort in the dark
You are the vine I reach for
You are the sunflower's breeze in my eyes

I became infatuated with her innocence,
caught in a web of mixed catastrophes
where the fixations turned into addictions
and the atmosphere drizzles joy and drops
of gratification, I surrendered to her penumbra,
I slipped into a haze of affection and lust

You are the sunset in my daydream
You are the enchanted sea of grace
You are the sunflower's breeze in my eyes

A delicate sound of a violin, where tragedies are
treasured
and the sounds of the wind seek out the mysteries of
the beloved rain
I woke up in verses where desire was a thousand
candles,
I venture intro the slipstream and wait until the
dragonflies
prowl for her shivering spirit

You are the exhilaration in my puzzle
You are the jewel in my obscure soul
You are the sunflower's breeze in my eyes

I find myself between the insatiable chapters
and the anxiety that twitches in the shade of the
ancient tree,
I continue to ink and pour out the heartache I once
ignored
forgive me twilight, I am fond of your crippled and
fractured stars
I will follow your smeared moon

You are the magic in my stratosphere
You are the sugar fascination in my carousel
You are the sunflower's breeze in my eyes

I whisper softly into your white knuckled storms,
I want to be your thunder and crave for you to be my
lightning,
I gasp on the devotion
and tenderness, I grasp for your fragile and
soothing reverberation,
I long for your rapture
and invincible glow, I will chase your gloom

You are the compassion that forever sits still
You are the scent that lingers on my skin
You are the sunflower's breeze in my eyes

BEAUTY OF REFLECTION

She became terrified of the
phantom in her vulnerability
She became terrified of the
truth that has a glass eye
She became terrified of the
sensitivity worn on her sleeve
She became terrified of the
villain that stalks her secrets

I fell in love with her reflection
even though she refuses to look
at herself in the mirror

"How can you love me
if all I see is ugly?"

I cherish what you can't see

She became terrified of the
firefly in her warm sympathy
She became terrified of the
fears that jittered in the dark
She became terrified of the
lies that spoke in the brilliance
She became terrified of the
pieces that dwell in her chaos

I fell in love with her reflection
even though she refuses to look
at herself in the mirror

"How can you love me
if all I see is pain?"

I cherish what you can't see

She became terrified of the
riddles in her echoing courage
She became terrified of the
anxiety scowling at her nerves
She became terrified of the
suspicion gnawing at her sleep
She became terrified of the
walls she harmlessly built

I fell in love with her reflection
even though she refuses to look
at herself in the mirror

"How can you love me
if all I see isn't enough?"

I cherish what you can't see

ONCE UPON A JAGGED STAR

Once upon a jagged star
I found a four-leaf clover dancing
in her auric hair, the serenity peaked
through the iron curtain seeking peace
I sought out tranquility within the
depths of the roundabout like observations
In the teeter totter of my perplexed mind
my castles in the air became flustered
the answers slipped from her pastoral lips
I begin to recognize my weaknesses
and her strengths outshined the ridged star
She became the luster in my universe

MELODY IN THE SAND

She stepped inside the watercolor
illusion with a glow of serendipity
dressed in charisma and sophistication
Strolling down, glaring at lucid memories
gawking at the fluffy still amusements

And the oblivion sheds its skin
And the hesitation quivers
And the skepticism is tarnished

As she walks in the bleached sand
a melody plays in her ear…
"Your beauty is in your scars"

She glides into the path of her equilibrium
a place of poise but gripping to the petals
of the rose, drops of self-worth falls to the floor
She can feel the details of sin disperse
carefully misguiding intuition and dignity

And the inward rejection resumes
And the perplexity simmers
And the uncertainty dangles

As she walks in the bleached sand
a melody plays in her ear…
"Your beauty is waltzing in your eyes"

She anxiously scratches at doubt with a penny
Quietly she writes in her burgundy diary
penning a letter to the light and absolute being
pursuing pillars of confidence and credence
digging for a black and white resolution

And the reluctance shimmers
And the suspicion trembles
And the disbelief shudders

As she walks in the bleached sand
a melody plays in her ear…
"Your beauty is parading within"

*The mirror can see
that you are as beautiful
as I do*

FOREVERMORE ENTWINED

Repeatedly, she is exceptionally pleasant
Periodically, she is dashing and divine
Consistently, she is punctual and independent
Constantly, she is kind-hearted and gentle
Frequently, she is considerate and tender

Forevermore, my heart is entwined with hers

Typically, she is good natured and authentic
Regularly, she is merciful and generous
Habitually, she is sympathetic and gracious
Customarily, she is courteous and courageous
Naturally, she is appealing and engaging

Forevermore, my heart is entwined with hers

Normally, she is forgiving and affectionate
Routinely, she is loyal and reverent
Usually, she is remarkable and caring
Ordinarily, she is thoughtful and devoted
Commonly, she is delightful and amiable

Forevermore, my heart is entwined with hers

NOVEMBER WIND

She crawled out from the nights that twist
and mirror distress

She crawled out of the gloom that
curved for endless miles

She crawled out from the obscurity
and the silence that screamed

Yet her fears disappeared and fell in love
with the November Wind

And she blossomed into something incredible

She crawled out from the slippery connotation
and the nerve-racking innuendos

She crawled out of the heinous remarks
and the bone chilling accusations

She crawled out of the insinuations with daggers
and the lustrous inferences

Yet her anxiety vanished and
fell in love with the November Wind

And she blossomed into something stunning

She crawled out of the blurred dungeon
and the paraphrases in bold ink

She crawled out of the state of indecision and
the spinning mindset

She crawled out of the nebulous shadow and
and broke away from the chains

Yet her anger melted and
fell in love with the November Wind

And she blossomed into something unbelievable

INVINCIBLE BLAZE

She has a blaze that is unable to be extinguished

She has a blaze that speaks invincibility and
is a gift

And she is my guiding light

She has a blaze that does not bend or
break among the ruins

She has a blaze that is unspoken and
never is restless

And she is my shimmering truth

She has a blaze that is fearless and
incredibly valiant

She has a blaze that is forgiving and
scorching beauty

And she is my concrete flower

She has a blaze that is fierce and
serenity dances on her fingertips

She has a blaze that doesn't have a shadow
or a flaw

And she is my magnificent wind

CRIMSON HILLS

I believe in your howling breeze that
wraps around my barricades
I believe in your words, suffering,
and the burning of your tongue
I believe in your sparkling eyelashes,
quiet prisoners, and summer ashes
I believe in your cities of glitter, spinning colors
and the ink fading in your diary

And we will walk hand in hand in the crimson hills
And I'm in love with your fortress
Forever, I will kiss your forehead in the rain

I believe in your graffiti on your walls on the inside
I believe in your spellbinding affection
and your breathtaking artistry
I believe in your tears of your daydreams
and the collision within
I believe in your earthquakes and
your rivers of devotion

And we will walk hand in hand in the crimson hills
And I'm in love with your embrace
Forever, I will crave your precious skin

I believe in your discolored reverence
and hollow dismay
I believe in your rust, bold convictions,
and your sleepless concerns
I believe in your masked intuition and
the darkness that surrounds your clouds
I believe in your clarity and your splash of purity

And we will walk hand in hand in the crimson hills
And I'm in love with your paradise
Forever, I will encircle your warmth

PINS AND NEEDLES

A very few want to see the colors
I drown myself in
A very few want to see my mascara
run down my alabaster skin
A very few want to love the bits
and fragments of me

In my pins and needles,
I appreciate your gentleness
I appreciate your affection

Love me as much as I adore you

A very few want to see the pages I've written
and read
A very few want to dip their feet
in my creek of agony
A very few want to stay and
hold my tired hands

Love me as much as I cherish you

In my pins and needles
I appreciate your comfort
I appreciate your warmth

A very few want to delve deeper
into the veins of my soul
A very few want to feel my invisible
and burnt scars
A very few want to understand my
sorrow and misfortunes

Love me as much as I savor you

In my pins and needles
I appreciate your grace
I appreciate your time

*I never sleep as good
with you not beside me*

CHARM FOR KEEPS

She's covered in a quilt of insecurities
She's covered with spots of trepidation

And yet I'm the one who is lucky

She's covered in silence and concern
She's covered with freckles of distress

And yet I'm the one who is lucky

She's covered in distrust and loss
She's covered with reluctance and confusion

And yet I'm the one who is lucky

She's covered in melancholy and fickle burns
She's covered with mystery and edges

And yet I'm the one who is lucky

TRUE DISTINCTION

I became a lost obligation
I became a trinket sitting on the shelf
I became a toy in the wrinkled sheets

But he pulls me in to hold me
But he doesn't just lust for my skin
But he treats me like gold
But he pulls me in so close
there isn't a gap of fear

A true distinction of a man and a boy

I became a figurine in your collection
I became a rendezvous in your shadows
I became a number one secret

But he plays with my fingertips
But he caresses me in the light
But he uses the word love
But he wipes away the sadness
there isn't any more tears

A true distinction of a man and a boy

UNDER THE ASH OAK TREE

Under the ash oak tree
I'm standing on my tippy toes reaching
for the longest hanging branch
As my fingers almost touched the limb
I fell to the flourishing grass
with my nose buried in the meadow
I found my heart dancing with glee
Everything in my life that I have ever touched
has no comparison to your embrace

NOVEMBER 4, 2008

I kissed your lips for the first time
and felt a chill travel down my spine
I savored the goosebumps
I knew it was the beginning of
something amazing and felt love echo
I embraced the tapestry
I didn't want to stop kissing you
I saw a glimpse of our future
within the melting of the ice
I saw skies open and felt
rain dance on my tongue
I was petrified and a part of me
was frozen but another
part was mesmerized
I knew when I placed my hand
on your cheek this was
meant to be forever

I kissed your lips for the first time
and felt a chill travel down my spine

PRECIOUS HONOR

I love you for the strong will you possess
I love you for the storms you weathered

Thank you for your grace

I love you for the mirror you barely glare into
I love you for the determination instilled

Thank you for your affection

I love you for the tenderness you carry
I love you for the education you have gained

Thank you for your spirit

I love you for the past you have walked through
I love you for the nights you've laid next to me

Thank you for your ablaze

I love you for the mornings I've held you close
I love you for being the light in the dark

Thank you for your patience

I love you for being everything I could imagine
I love you for being the beginning and my end

AUTUMN KISS

Leaves of aggravation blew away
Leaves of complexity flew away

Leaves of illusions blew away
Leaves of affliction flew away

Your autumn kiss saved my burning soul

Leaves of fragments blew away
Leaves of agony flew away

Leaves of misfortune blew away
Leaves of catastrophe flew away

Your autumn kiss saved my blistering soul

Leaves of emptiness blew away
Leaves of hopelessness flew away

Leaves of heartache blew away
Leaves of solitude flew away

Your autumn kiss saved my smoldering soul

*I fell in love
with your heart
before I fell in love
with your body*

UNSEEN DIAMOND

She pronounces herself as a battle
of a thousand scratches
She pronounces herself as a heart full of
thorns and roses dipped in ink

I found her to be endearing
a peacemaker, treasurable, and a diamond

She pronounces herself as an exhausted vase
waiting for a bouquet of wishes
She pronounces herself as a backbreaker
with invisible bruises

I found her to be captivating
a patient needleworker, priceless and transcendent

She pronounces herself as a star gazer with
theories bitten by crooked teeth
She pronounces herself as a burned out
magician with sterling wings

I found her to be spellbinding
a summer's wind, delightful and gleaming

FOG OF SORROW

She knuckled down on being persistent
and trustworthy
She knuckled down on peeling
the layers of bloodless skin
She knuckled down on discovering her inner key

And the fog of sorrow vanished
And the dreams within glistened
And the heartache faded

I found the change to be adorable

She knuckled down on gripping onto faith
and throwing away hostility
She knuckled down on being rational and
stared into the bright colors of her emotions
She knuckled down on healing and
the twinkling transitions

And the fog of sorrow disappeared
And the nightmares within became dim
And the agony became dull

I found the change to be charming

DRIPPING SINCERITY

I can feel your apology
within your tears of your sincerity
I can feel the threshold
of your tender sincerity

And I fell harder within your vulnerability

I can feel your confession within
your drops of your sincerity
I can feel your compassion
drown in your sincerity

And I fell harder within your vulnerability

I can feel your affection within
the sparkle of your sincerity
I can feel your rainbows twinkling
within your sincerity

And I fell harder within your vulnerability

UNTAMED SCARS

She spoke with a fragment of her mind
She spoke with volumes of her heart
She spoke with patience spinning
from her tongue

And she turned the corner into another
chapter with conviction
And she fell in love with her
untamed scars even more

She spoke with a spit of determination
and a cup of gumption
She spoke with a blemish of fear
and an ounce of doubt
She spoke with a flavor of tact and
a pinch of grace

And she turned the corner into another
chapter with confidence
And she fell in love with her
untamed scars even more

She spoke with veins of consideration
She spoke with crooning good intentions
She spoke with gospel tattooed on her wrists

And she turned the corner into another
chapter with faith
And she fell in love with her
untamed scars even more

SLEEPING IN PEACE

Peacefully,
she fell asleep in my arms
Peacefully,
she felt my shadows glisten
Peacefully,
she wrapped her strength around me
Peacefully,
she listened to my heartbroken song
Peacefully,
she wiped away my tears
Peacefully,
she made me complete
Peacefully,
she had sewn up my pieces

TEARS OF JOY

I prayed for someone to hold me,
there she stood
I prayed for someone to love me,
there she was

And I embrace my tears of joy

I prayed for someone to understand me,
there she is
I prayed for someone to appreciate me,
there she sat

And I embrace my tears of joy

I prayed for someone to guide me,
there she stayed
I prayed for someone to fulfill my dreams,
there she lives

And I embrace my tears of joy

I love
the depths
of the ocean
in your
eyes

THE BACKBONE'S SIGH

She use to let hope
slip through the cracks
She use to let castles
slip through the cracks

In the crevice she discovered
her moonlit backbone

And I sigh from her strength

She use to let fear
slip through the cracks
She use to let anguish
slip through the cracks

In the crevice she discovered
her silvery backbone

And I sigh from the light

She use to let affection
slip through the cracks
She use to let desire
slip through the cracks

In the crevice she discovered
her twinkling backbone

And I sigh from her magic

SUNSET'S FLAME

When the night falls
I lean in to hear your name
I lean in to feel your distinction

Deep into the sunrise,
I cry for your presence

When the night falls
I lean in to take in your rhapsody
I lean in to gather your pieces

Deep into the sunrise,
I cry for your wisdom

Thank you for being the sunset's flame

When the night falls
I lean in to awaken your shade
I lean in to treasure your ambience

Deep into the sunrise,
I cry for your devotion

When the night falls
I lean in to drown in your scent
I lean in to engrave my dreams

Thank you for being the sunset's flame

LOVE AND SORROW

For you, love, and sorrow
melts away the snow in the raging winter
I've seen admiration bellow from the
empty sky and my heartache entwine
with rain and the promises, he once gave

The love he wrote between the verses
became stale, tired, and thin like paper
The love I whisper between the chatter
becomes cemented as I graze your cheek

I will give you one real flower than the fake
dozen that you didn't feel

For you, love, and sorrow
is a shadow chained to yesterday's wishes
I've seen adoration smolder in the kisses
of the wind and my fears ripple in the calm
I am not the deceiver and trickster he was

The sorrow he left leaves a splotchy stain,
an aftertaste, and anxiety crawling up and down
The sorrow he gave is a remainder and a reminder,
quietly bleeding within

I will give you vulnerability, truth, and
a jagged past that screams real

FLY WITH ME, MY LOVE

I will forever kiss your lost paradigm
I will forever kiss your ballet shoes
I will forever kiss your violin strings

Fly with me, my love

I will forever kiss your sea of hallucinations
I will forever kiss your lucent philosophy
I will forever kiss your complex patterns

Fly with me, my love

I will forever kiss your yearn for knowledge
I will forever kiss your isosceles theories
I will forever kiss your tenacity and hunger

Fly with me, my love

I will forever kiss your abundance of joy
I will forever kiss your lightning and thunder
I will forever kiss your desolate paintings

Fly with me, my love

I will forever kiss your frazzled wings
I will forever kiss your fields of animation
I will forever kiss your candlelit tales

Fly with me, my love

UNDER YOUR CHARMING SPELL

I've been drowning
in your courageous mystique
I've been drowning
in your comical inner child

And I follow the perfume,
Under your charming spell

I've been drowning
in your prismatic sagacity
I've been drowning
in your misguided wreckage

And I follow your lead,
Under your charming spell

I've been drowning
in your wildfire like atmosphere
I've been drowning
in your magnificent desire

And I follow your center,
Under your charming spell

I've been drowning
in your unbiased points of view
I've been drowning
in your twitching superstition

And I follow your melody,
Under your charming spell

TWO O'CLOCK BISTRO

Sapphire eyes shifting to the left
in the Chardonnay air, quietly humming a
melody, slightly neurotic but magnetic,
staring into her sunny side spring salad,
gazing at her soft alabaster skin,
exchanging sarcastic one liner, chuckling
over circus like jokes, stumbling into
a conversation of psychology, the sound of
delicate piano prancing in our ears,
comforting and pleasant, a first date,
surveying her countless layers, probing
her intuition and critical thinking, analytics
spinning in her octagon, appreciation her
fondness of classical music, fumbling into
the intensity of Ayn Rand, dissecting "The
Fountainhead" with an exceptional view,
A beautiful glimpse of the Two O'clock Bistro

*I
wouldn't
be
where
I am
today
without
you*

WATERCOLOR'S TEARS

I've seen your transcribed tears
and my insides are silent in the birdcage

I've heard your softhearted endeavors
and my insides inhale your symmetry

And I love the colors in your painting

I've seen your hemorrhaging atmosphere
and my insides will weep your name

I've heard your whirlwind howl
and my insides are awakened from your shine

And I love the vault in your painting

I've seen your sublime crown
and my insides are provoked from your voice

I've heard your parade of storms
and my insides are waiting for your retiring

And I love the view in your painting

UNBROKEN

With you,
there are no omissions and pauses in the dark

With you,
clarity and unison glide in our pristine air

I feel complete

With you,
balance is refreshing and softening

With you,
there are no faults and quirks that are sleeping

I feel whole

With you,
trust is a boulder with our hands around it

With you,
love is natural and free like a bird

I feel undivided

With you,
there are no doubts and worry floating around your
neck

With you,
safety and peace are a reality, no longer a wish or a
dream

I feel unbroken

BURNING SHADOWS

I use to collect ancient coins, irrational dreams,
and water downed books of passion

I use to carry a bag of anxiety, suitcase of apologies
and excuses in my pockets

And you have burned my shadows with your
treasured love
I see love in a new light

I use to displace anger, bottles of emptiness and
was thirsty for endless amounts of affection

I use to channel ignorance in crevices and
hide behind my faults

And you have burned my shadows with your
treasured love
I see love with new eyes

I use to stare into the talking voids and
the piles of empathy

I use to chase untamed fantasies, sinister pleasures,
and unrecognizable lies

And you have burned my shadows
with your treasured love

I see love with a new point of view

ENGRAVED MEMORIES

I haven't forgotten
about the nights filed with laughter
I haven't forgotten
about the conversations filled with wonder

The memories are engraved within

I haven't forgotten
about the treasurable mornings
I haven't forgotten
about the paradise in your touch

The memories are engraved within

I haven't forgotten
about the landscape of our first kiss
I haven't forgotten
about the flowers in our garden

The memories are engraved within
I haven't forgotten
about you the day you said "I do"
I haven't forgotten
about the magic between us

The memories are engraved within

FOR YOU AND THE TRUTH

For you and the truth,
I lay awake circling my vulnerability
I can taste the poison on my tongue
I dwell in my pond of insecurities
I gnaw at my unspoken and sedated soul
I claw at my resilience with my tired fingers
I pick at my invisible wounds with an axe
I watch the apprehension hang over my head
I whisper to my demons "listen to the crack"

I am holding your hand with one eye open
a gust of change feels like a storm
I'm terrified to open both eyes
to see I don't deserve you

For you and the truth,
I find myself misplaced and disoriented
I spot the conditions and uncontrollable urges
I removed the hindering spotlight
I am haunted by my effervescent carnival
I have waved goodbye to the magnetic carousel
I steer toward the corridor of isolation
I clutch on to the paradise dancing in your eyes
I am sinking in the malevolent circus

I am holding your hand with one eye open
a gust of change feels like a storm
I'm terrified to open both eyes
to see I don't deserve you

For you and the truth,
I am weeping on the inside in this masquerade
I am praying I will find edges of my identity
I leave my pieces behind reaching for you
I grip on to tomorrow and replay yesterdays
I cough up the suffocating air and sorrow
I choke on my frustrations and crooked thunder

I see the lightning in my affliction
I recognize the heartache that flickers within

I am holding your hand with one eye open
a gust of change feels like a storm
I'm terrified to open both eyes
to see I don't deserve you

You are everything
I could want and more

LOVE IS A FLOWER

Without tenderness and comfort
we won't grow
Without compassion and understanding
we won't grow
Without mistakes and flaws
we won't grow
Without clarity and warmth
we won't grow
Without passion and tears of affection
we won't grow
Without sunlight and rain
we won't grow
Without dreams and support
we won't grow

COMPLETE

When we were apart
I felt lost and confused
When we were apart
I lied awake and couldn't sleep

Together I feel whole

When we were apart
I felt something missing
When we were apart
I felt the pieces tremble

Together I feel peace

When we were apart
I felt hollow and empty
When we were apart
I felt lonely and incomplete

Together I feel whole

PERFECT TO ME

You don't need to lose
an ounce of weight
You don't need to hide
your quirks and flaws

You feel perfect to me

You don't need eyeliner
or mascara on your face
You don't need to hold
on to your fears and past

You feel perfect to me

I DO

When the sky is gray and revolting
I lean on you
When the night is somber and fearless
I trust your intuition
When the light fades and darkness spreads
I embrace your affection
When the morning cracks and sings
I reach for your delicate hands
When the glow evaporates, and troubles linger
I rest my head on your shoulder
When the emptiness and tears collide
I melt in your comforting arms
When the minister stands before us
I say "I do" with joy dancing inside my soul

FOR ME, THE SELFISH

For me, the selfish
I want all your electrifying skin to myself
Inhaling your mind, cynicism and
charm to dance around your lips
I am on my knees at your wonder
awestruck and guided by your intuition

I am self-indulgent when it comes to your desires
I am self-indulgent when it comes to your wishes

For me, the selfish
I want your affection and castles to breathe
gasping for your dazzling language
entwined with your fluorescent storytelling,
flickering philosophies, off-color dreams
I am hungry for your honey like fascination

I am self-indulgent when it comes to your candy
I am self-indulgent when it comes to your insatiable
flames

For me, the Selfish,
I want your closeness to transform my edges,
wrapped around my screams soothing me,
admiring your brilliance and path
I am enthusiastic for your excellence
your candor and style consume me

I am self-indulgent when it comes to your mind
I am self-indulgent when it comes to your essence

SANGUINE COLORED WISHES

Staring into a mystic daydream
Longing for my muse to feel my aches
Burning agony runs down my throat
Sensitivity bursting and echoing
Provocative sanguine colored wishes cry
Fingerprints steaming in the garden
Overtaken by the shadows of desire
Decorations surrounding the inferno
Sparks and smoke tangle up in our haze
Condensation falling on her forehead
Watercolors of this rhythmic scene
Moisture seeking traces of magic
Shaking and sweating with intensity
Never ending appetite for a fever

*I get teary eyed
every time
I hear our song*

A ROSY GLOW AT DAWN

Painting a distinctive glow
Obscurity of a blazing orange
A tint of a brilliant glare
Brush strokes with preciousness
A scent of simple radiance
Charisma and chemistry sing
A balance of purity and symbolism
Refined and burnished with charm
Prestige colors magnified
Hands of dexterity shimmering
A state of majesty and perfection
Watching through a glass ocean
Love and appreciation mending
A plethora of burnt stars in the galaxy
Waving to the tears of the moon
An artist sketching a dream from
The inside of a haunting nightmare
Wiping away the sadness with her brush

UNBLEMISHED

You are perfect for my sentimental heart
You are perfect for my barricades with glitter
You are perfect for my weary tongue
You are perfect for my untamed throat

Hand in hand, you are unblemished

You are perfect for my freckled wrinkles
You are perfect for my scattered mind
You are perfect for my scarlet wounds
You are perfect for my darkest secrets

Hand in hand, you are unblemished

You are perfect for my stray sins
You are perfect for my seas without a sun
You are perfect for my abandoned vase
You are perfect for my brisk despair

Hand in hand, you are unblemished

BLESSED

I love the woman that you were
I love the woman that isn't afraid
I love the woman that speaks up

I couldn't be any more blessed

I love the woman that embraces her scars
I love the woman that sparkles in the dark
I love the woman that lights up my universe

I couldn't be any more blessed

I love the woman that seizes the moment
I love the woman that isn't scared to death
I love the woman that you have become

I couldn't be any more blessed

YOU ARE MY OXYGEN

You are my oxygen
and have falling in love with the air
You are my oxygen
and in awe with the atmosphere

You are my oxygen
and embrace the sounds of the music box
You are my oxygen
and I am entwined with your spirit

You are my oxygen
and can feel you in my lungs
You are my oxygen
and my soul feels light as a balloon

You are my oxygen
and I feel incredibly alive
You are my oxygen
and terrified I can't get enough

LESSONS OF THE SOUL

She taught me the ways of the wind
She taught me to swim in the deep
and darkest oceans
She taught me to dream in a world
of takers and thieves
She taught me to love
with an inquisitive eye
She taught me how to give with
clarity with naked gestures

And the lessons of the soul make me tremble

She taught me to appreciate my losses
and accept my wounds
She taught me to walk with the breeze
and embrace the leaves of the fall
She taught me to speak with intentions
and leave agendas behind
She taught me how to love with
her precious and sacred heart
She taught me to be a man of my word

And the lessons of the soul make me cautious

She taught me to hold on to the memories
that dance in the twilight
She taught me how to inhale the
beauty of the seasons
She taught me to how to love
from the center of my heart
She taught me how to let go and
wrap my arms around her vulnerability
She taught me to how to grow a flower
with patience and tears of strength

And the lessons of the soul make me the man I am
today

*I love
the determination and strength
in your voice*

ESSENCE

Love me like the sand loves the footprints
Love me like the sky loves the clouds

Love me like the canvas loves the colors
Love me like the trees loves the leaves

I am madly in love with your essence

Love me like the flowers loves the petals
Love me like the earth loves the rain

Love me like the notebook loves the ink
Love me like the eyes loves the tears

I am madly in love with your essence

Love me like the lips loves the kisses
Love me like the lungs loves the air

Love me like the hands loves the touch
Love me like the eyes loves the view

I am madly in love with your essence

Love me like the sky loves the stars
Love me like the ocean loves the fishes

Love me like the skin loves the bones
Love me like the darkness loves the light

I am madly in love with your essence

AT LAST, MY VALENTINE

At last, my valentine,
the nightfall is brimming with endearment
whirlwind of emotion, sanctified caress
blossoming affection, flourishing scent
a rapture with a crimson glow
serenity spoken with a delicate accent
kindness spilling from your lips
love is no longer obscure nor a shadow
surrounded by peace, shimmering harmony
desire is not a color of lust, engraved souls
certainty is intertwined, respect is gilded
your halo sparkles and the hurricane fades

STILL

Despite the friction and imperfections
I am still drawn to you

Despite the colorless facade
I am still captivated by you

Despite the many that broke your heart
I am still enchanted by you

Despite what you see in the mirror
I am still enthralled by you

Despite the hurdles you throw at me
I am still magnetized to you

Despite all that we have endured
I am still in love with you

5:15 AM

At 5:15
I leaned in closer in the dark
Breathing in her scent
ecstatic I lay next to her every day
listening to the light sleeper
silently appreciating the moment
reflecting on the years and memories
our song playing in my head
entranced by the love we share
I fall in love all over again

I discovered peace
when I found you

FROM THE MOMENT WE MET

From the moment we met,
we were never strangers
From the moment we met,
we were never far apart

I felt something extraordinary

From the moment we met,
we sprinkled joy and laughter
From the moment we met,
we sipped on a glass of romance

I felt something miraculous

From the moment we met,
we swam in a river of peace
From the moment we met,
we slept in a world of love

I felt something worth keeping

BESIDE ME

Tomorrow will be
delightful and full of decorated promise
Tomorrow will be
savory with a pinch of generosity

Beside me is a future with you

Tomorrow will be
filled with flavor and dripping moons
Tomorrow will be
effervescent with a splash of tenderness

Beside me is a strong and soft hand

Tomorrow will be
glistening and saturated with peace
Tomorrow will be
blissful with a hint of compassion

Beside me is a never-ending light

MOTHER OF MY CHILD

The mother of my child
is consistently run down and tired
The mother of my child
is incredibly patient and a sweet pear

The mother of my child
is astonishingly forgiving and soft hearted
The mother of my child
is full of endless love and affection

The mother of my child
is a luminous humanitarian
The mother of my child
is endearing and tender in the center

The mother of my child
is nature's companion and quilt
The mother of my child
is the fortress and my sweet kingdom

The mother of my child
is a woman of pure distinction
The mother of my child
is everything I could imagine and more

SKIN OF COURAGE

I see the beauty in your
mysterious scars and tragedies
I see the beauty in your
self-doubt and inquisitions

And I'm no longer afraid
of your skin of courage

I see the beauty in your
lion like strength and battles
I see the beauty in your
vulnerability and devotion

And I'm no longer afraid
of your skin of courage

I see the beauty in your
wildfire and serene reflections
I see the beauty in your
steel fists and determination

And I'm no longer afraid
of your skin of courage

I see the beauty in your
valiant torch and pale reverence
I see the beauty in your
tears of the untouchable blaze

And I'm no longer afraid
of your skin of courage

THE GIFT

Visually she's perfect from head to toe
She has twinkling eyes that shine like diamonds
She has a smile that glows everlasting
She has a fun-loving spirit that should be embraced
by all
She has a dynamic style that makes her special
To know her is a gift and a blessing

She has a smell that is intoxicating that I am
drowning in
She is a classic and full of vibrating joy
She is a rare breed of women and is simply unique
She has a skin of gold and is priceless jewel
She is sweet brown sugar with a dab of spice
To know her is a gift and a blessing

Visually she is stimulating to the eyes
She has a walk that leaves me catatonic
She has a captivating mind and a gravitating soul
She is the center of what is pure and true
She is a statue of beauty and elegance
God must have taken his time with her
To know her is a gift and a blessing

She is an aphrodisiac and addicting to the eyes
She is a dream come true
She is something you don't find every day
She makes the world go round with her presence
She is amazing and I am in awe
To know her is a gift and a blessing

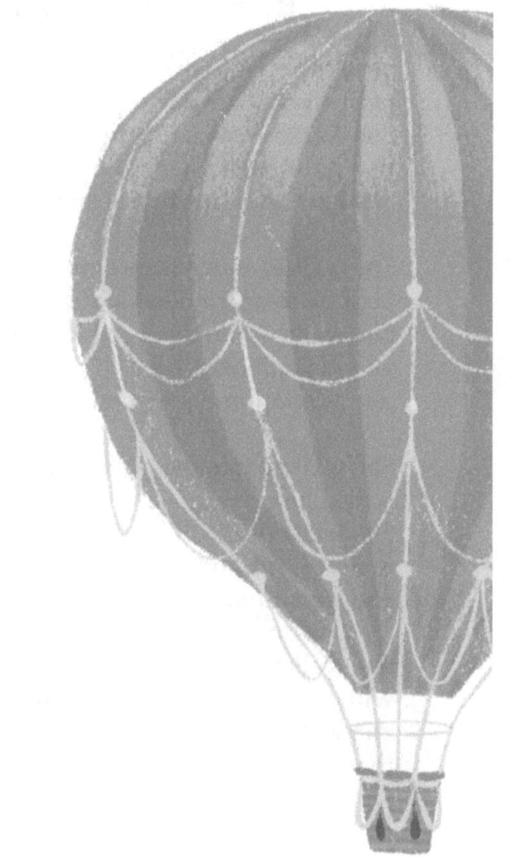

*My life
begins
and ends
with you*

BEAUTIFULLY BROKEN

She walked into the rhythm
of the unspoken dance
She walked into a breeze
that illuminated her glow
She left California to feel another sun

She walked into a haze that
became clear from her scars
She walked into the word loyalty
and never looked back
She left happiness without a choice

She walked into the phrase "come here"
with a luscious smile
She walked into the candles of hope
to give her a glimpse of her future
She left summer to stand in a chill

She walked into the morning rain
without an umbrella to embrace the sensitivity
She walked into a pale sky seeking colors
that would make her stronger
She left a chapter struggling to turn the pages
still looking beautiful

TERMS OF ENDEARMENT

It's been a pleasure, my love
It's been a joy, my sweetheart

You are my center

It's been a delight, my plum
It's been wondrous, my beloved

You are my rock

It's been precious, my sweet pea
It's been a dreamscape, my angel

You are my other half

It's been enchanting, my dear
It's been a world of glee, my light

You are my world

OCEAN OF ROMANCE

If we could ever make love
She would get all my attention
I could ensure rhythm, melody, and harmony
Our world would contain passion and respect
I don't lust for you, I adore you

We would melt in the unfounded fire
The wind that surrounds us seems to have no direction
You can step your foot into the waters of peace
I won't let you drown in the ocean of romance
Let me show you how the world should really be
I can give you something to embrace and believe

If you could ever let me kiss her lovely lips,
She could feel how much I cherish her as a person
I could ensure enriched love, perfection, and treasures
Our world would possess serenity and loyalty
I don't lust for you, I crave you

We would vanish as our delicate souls emerge as one
The clouds that are above us seem to open up
You can step your foot into the waters of peace,
I won't let you drown in the ocean of romance.
Let me show you how the world should really be
I can give you something to embrace and believe

If you could ever feel the touch of my hands,
She could see that all her grace that sits on a pedestal
I could ensure magic, warmth, and comfort
Our world would latch on to balance and patience
I don't lust for you, I glorify you

We would grasp on the ropes of love and affection.
The scenery is gleaming with trust
You can step your foot into the waters of peace
I won't let you drown in the ocean of romance
Let me show you how the world should really be
I can give you something to embrace and believe

FOREHEAD KISS

Vigorously illuminating
She's overworked
Quite compelling
She's overtired
Completely potent
She's giving
Magically robust
She's asleep on the couch
Forever lovely
She's precious
Make-up less
She's still captivating
Deserves everything
She deserves a forehead kiss

STARK RAVING ARMOR

She fell in love
with his top hat and vaudeville looks
She fell in love
with his chocolate wit and ripped edge tone
She fell in love
with his Broadway voice and commanding demeanor
She fell in love
with his gloss and glitz of his sword
She fell in love with
his gallant worth and the backbone of his confidence
She fell in love
with his chivalry and gentle heart
She fell in love
with his deep river and his stark raving armor
She fell in love
with his lyrics and got lost in the melody

You are the melody
in our song

TENDER AND RARE

I could easily fall
for the moon in your twinkling eyes
I could easily fall
for your precious skin

I could easily fall
for your soothing heavenly voice
I could easily fall
for the stars above your head

I could easily fall
for your gentle and warm touch
I could easily fall
for the sweetness on your lips

I could easily fall
for the world held in your palm
I could easily fall
for your charm and wit

I could easily fall
for your enticing sigh
I could easily fall
into your delicate universe

GORGEOUS MAKES ME CRAZY

Staring at your vivid portrait
Awestruck and floating butterflies
soaring in my stomach
Tingling sensations in my bones
Enamored with your animated spirit
Full of zest and enthusiasm
A wondrous and gentle endearment
Voluptuous from head to toe
Captivating to the delicate core
Amazed by your enticing hurricane
Hot-blooded and seductive
Drawn to your language and accent
Gorgeous makes me crazy

THE FRAGILE PRIZE

Sentiments drifting in a box
Grappling with drops of emptiness
Reflections of glee captured
A gem restoring faith and hope

Polishing off the elegant rust
Refined and forever blooming
Treasuring the memoirs
A jewel gleaming in the dark

Unnoticed but unblemished
Speckless on the inside
Crystal vase held by miraculous hands
An ornament made up of untarnished pearls

IN A GARDEN OF REMEMBRANCE

In a garden of remembrance
under a blinking and winter moon
that reveals your beauty
our love shimmers and blossoms
Inhaling your joyful smile
memories guiding me to your heart
seeking a resting place of tranquility

In a garden of remembrance
I found a shadow and light
that reveals your beauty
our love sparkles and glistens
Exhaling your graceful spirit
memories flowing like a river to your heart
residing in your sensitive arms

COLORS OF TREASURE

Love my blackened scars
Love my lopsided flaws
Love my fatal quirks
Love my enigmatic perception

Thank you for loving me

Love my complicated essence
Love my simple comforter
Love my undying will
Love my quivering fears

Thank you for loving me

Love my shadow's tears
Love my effervescent soul
Love my conflicted backbone
Love my distinctive complexion

Thank you for loving me

I gazed into her clouds
as I consumed her rain

GLAMOROUS SKIN

She plays the cello with strings
from her smooth heart
She sings with enormous strength
yet carries a lullaby in her throat
and she doesn't see herself blossom
She writes poetry with a sunflower in her hand
She hangs between the sparkles and limelight
and she doesn't see the jewels
She speaks with benevolence and shimmering grace
She composes luscious creations with her fingertips
and she doesn't hear the invigorating encore
She serenades to the delightful ears
She is a beauty that never stops illuminating
and she doesn't feel the glamour
on her skin she deserves

PRECIOUS LOVE

Your eyes are filled
with a euphoric sea
Your innocent smile
makes me full
Your laughter
tickles my soul
Your curiosity
is adorably cute
Your persistence is
remarkable and
Your face is a precious gift
I love all of you so much

LONGING FOR FOREVERMORE

I'm longing for over the top devotion
I'm longing for the missing to be an ache

I'm longing for the colors to feel bright
I'm longing for the tears in your eyes

I'm longing for the touch to make me quiver
I'm longing for the kiss to never stop

I'm longing for the words you say to shout
I'm longing for the actions to match your words

I'm longing for the desire to be overwhelming
I'm longing for the gap between us to disappear

I'm longing for us to mean what we stated in our vows
I'm longing for the word forever to be inscribed in
our veins

LOVING YOU

I can only give you what you want
if you speak your mind
I can only give you what you need
if you speak up

I can only love all of you
if you share all of yourself
I can only give you what you want
if you open up

I can only give you what you need
If you reveal your true self
I can only love all of you
if you release the beauty inside

I can only give you what you want
if you show me who you are
I can only give you want you need
if you throw away your fears

I can only love all of you
if you let me see the real you

You made me
believe
love existed

BEDAZZLED BY BEAUTY

I found elegance when I walked into the room
Mesmerized
I found treasure when I fell into her melodic eyes
Awestruck
I found heaven when I saw her magnificent face
Hypnotized

I found a goddess when I felt a chill run down my
spine
Fascinated
I found grace when a bolt of thunder soared through
my veins
Captivated
I found perfection in this astonishing angel from
above
Raptured

I found joy when her smile gave me shivers
Entranced
I found rainbows when serenity glided from her
heart
Bedazzled
I found beauty when she released her wit and charm
Amazed

CHERISHING YOU

I cherished the rose petals that
paraded in her afterglow
I cherished the softness that
stood still on her cheeks
Our love felt like a dream

I cherished the happiness that
smelled like perfume
I cherished the smile that never
left the carnival in my mind
Our love felt like a fairy tale

I cherished the innocence and the sugar
that fused under the moonlight
I cherished the watercolors that
fell from her precious sky
Our love felt like a rainbow

I cherished the harmony and kindness
that I felt from her kiss
I cherished the light and dark
that she cradled forevermore
Our love felt like it would never die

REKINDLED

Never underestimate
the voltage of affection
Revitalized

Never fear the force
of precious sentiments
Rejuvenated

Never be afraid
of the overwhelming tears
Reborn

Never neglect the seeds
of devotion
Reinvigorated

Never ignore the moments
that you once embraced
Reclaim

Never give up on love

PLEASE

Please
Be delicate if you hug her

Please
Be sincere if you say those three words

Please
Be gentle if you truly love her

Please
Be intuitive if you want to understand her

Please
Be everything to her if you want her

EVERLASTING GAZE

I see paradise in your
endearing photograph
Can't stop looking at you

I see utopia on your
alluring lipstick
Can't stop looking at you

I see the garden of Eden
in your mystical eyes
Can't stop looking at you

I see milk and honey
from head to toe
Can't stop looking at you

I see perfection and
and everlasting desire for you
Never will I stop
looking at you

9 781734 749984